ARTISTS AT HOME

· INSPIRED IDEAS FROM THE HOMES OF NEW MEXICO ARTISTS ·

BY EMILY DRABANSKI
FOREWORD BY ELMO BACA

Author: Emily Drabanski
Editor: Ree Strange Sheck
Copy Editor: Walter K. Lopez
Book Design & Production: Bette Brodsky
Publisher: Ethel Hess

FRONT MATTER PHOTO CREDITS:
Title Page: Tavlos art (Mark Nohl)
Page 2: Luis Tapia door (Steve Larese)
Page 4: Luis Tapia artwork (Steve Larese)
Page 5: Chair – Tapia/Padilla home (Steve Larese)

Library of Congress PCN Number: 2002115831
ISBN: 0-937206-66-0
Printed in China

ARTISTS AT HOME

· INSPIRED IDEAS FROM THE HOMES OF NEW MEXICO ARTISTS ·

BY EMILY DRABANSKI
FOREWORD BY ELMO BACA

TABLE OF

CONTENTS

FOREWORD

Few places seem to resonate with the rarified and subtle energies that an artist's personal quarters have. Creating art requires considerable personal adjustments of architecture, furnishings, lifestyle and attitude to achieve that state of grace that allows the creative spirit to soar free.

Art history (and I include all creative endeavors such as music, literature and the visual arts) is made more intimate and personal to us by the living spaces and personal effects left behind by creators.

Preserving artists' homes and studios is a recent and modern notion, greatly accelerated by the tourism industry, mass media and a global cult of celebrity.

The great sculptor Auguste Rodin's mansion/studio in Paris and Rembrandt's Amsterdam town house are national shrines and tourist must-sees. Houses of contemporary artists Frida Kahlo and Georgia O'Keeffe have also become pilgrimage destinations.

New Mexico has been widely acknowledged as one of the nation's leading art centers (No. 2 or 3, depending on the survey and source), and so it naturally harbors artists' dwellings of astonishing variety, ingenuity, wit and drama. Emily Drabanski has selected some of the best contemporary examples and lovingly interpreted them here to be savored over and over again, as they should be. This collection of homes speaks to and of gracious and inspired creative lifestyles in the arid high desert of New Mexico, and the homes embody enduring architectural themes.

The components of New Mexico's artistic and architectural heritage are well-known (the so-called three cultures of Native American, Hispanic and Anglo) and contribute heavily to the human environments celebrated in *Artists at Home*. A certain devotion to the rich artistic folklore of the region is made manifest in the rooms depicted here; deep respect for the Navajo weaver or Pueblo potter or Hispanic *santero* is often a point of departure for a color scheme or piece of furniture or maybe just an intended mood.

Despite its rich cultural antecedents, New Mexico was usually considered an isolated cultural backwater until professional artists and writers discovered it a century ago. The initial renaissance was led by Taos Society of Artists' founder Ernest L. Blumenschein, who enthusiastically recruited other talented friends such as Eanger Irving Couse, Joseph Henry Sharp, William H. "Buck" Dunton, E. Martin Hennings, Bert G. Phillips, Victor Higgins and many others to northern New Mexico. By 1920, both Taos and Santa Fe

THE BLUMENSCHEIN HOME AND MUSEUM IN TAOS REMAINS MUCH LIKE IT WAS WHEN ERNEST L. BLUMENSCHEIN LIVED THERE. ART AND FINE EUROPEAN AND SPANISH COLONIAL-STYLE ANTIQUES FILL THE HOME. (MARK NOHL PHOTO)

had become home to a galaxy of stellar talents.

Ever since the U.S. Army married Greek revival style to adobe architecture in the 1850s (producing the Territorial style), classical and Victorian details had begun to transform simple adobe houses into fascinating hybrids. Artists, however, brought their uncanny visual sophistication, eclecticism and considerable risk taking and daring to the organic, earthen architecture they loved. Their bohemian

ARTISTS REGULARLY GATHERED AT MABEL DODGE LUHAN'S HOUSE IN TAOS. (PHOTO CIRCA 1925, COURTESY YALE COLLECTION OF AMERICAN LITERATURE, BEINECKE LIBRARY, YALE UNIVERSITY)

O'Keeffe, D.H. Lawrence, Nicolai Fechin, Alice Corbin, William Penhallow Henderson and many others. To study their fine art and literature is to discover a mother lode of American genius. To study their homes is to discover how mundane, everyday existence is made authentic and extraordinary.

Artists being artists, it is often difficult to categorize their homes into overarching themes. Drabanski has provided us here with an excellent conceptual framework with which to tour and understand the distinctive homes of some of the state's leading artists. Certain interiors defy classification. Often a room's best and intangible qualities are products of refined sensibilities and strongly reflect the personalities and experiences of their designers.

I have often thought of writer and art patron Mabel Dodge Luhan's house in Taos as a unique New Mexican villa, grand in the European manner of scale and siting but organic and free-flowing in the Pueblo tradition. Personal extravagances and dec-

philosophy of the pursuit of art at all costs is what truly transformed Santa Fe and Taos into compelling towns and inspired homes of unforgettable beauty and power.

The first great generation of New Mexico bohemian artists and writers was active from about 1900 to World War II and included well-known personalities such as Blumenschein, Mabel Dodge Luhan, Witter Bynner, Ansel Adams, Georgia

orative whims (such as a curved, two-story adobe staircase leading to Mabel's private suite or the bathroom windows that D.H. Lawrence and Dorothy Brett painted) embellish the architecture in ways that transcend mere aesthetics.

Russian artist Nicolai Fechin created a home in Taos that is a synthesis of Russian folk design, adobe construction and virtuoso carpentry and woodworking. Virtually hand-crafted by Fechin himself, the house is a unique statement in the vast New Mexico architectural canon, and the built-in cabinetry he created continues to astound scholars and designers.

In retrospect the 1920s and 1930s were especially fertile years for the often-unpredictable circumstances where genius, money, culture and eccentricity interact in such a way as to produce remarkable homes. Alongside Mabel and Fechin in Taos, the bohemian group in Santa Fe was led by poet Witter Bynner, artist-designer William Penhallow Henderson and his wife, poet Alice Corbin, and society sisters Amelia and Martha White.

Bynner's sprawling estate on Old Santa Fe Trail grew from a tiny, two-room adobe hut to an undu-

NICOLAI FECHIN'S HOME REFLECTED HIS LOVE OF NEW MEXICO AND HIS RUSSIAN HOMELAND. THE FECHIN INSTITUTE MANAGES THE MAGNIFICENT PROPERTY, WHICH IS FILLED WITH FECHIN'S HAND-CRAFTED WOODWORK. (MARK NOHL PHOTO)

NICOLAI FECHIN INCLUDED THIS ALCOVE IN HIS TAOS HOME, A FEATURE POPULAR THROUGHOUT RUSSIA. (MARK NOHL PHOTO)

lating mass of rooms held together by a central two-story portal and balcony. Bynner was sure to build enough nooks and niches to accommodate both his impressive collection of Chinese art and guests from his overflow parties (Bynner's martinis and piano routines were legendary). An essential consideration of the artist's home is how well it protects privacy as well as how graciously it can offer spontaneous hospitality.

While not artists themselves, Amelia and Martha White generously supported art and cultural life in Santa Fe for many years and fully espoused a creative lifestyle. Their impressive compound on Garcia Street consisted of a classic two-story *sala* (large living room), complete with an orchestra balcony, where the sisters hosted refined cocktail and costume parties. On the grounds were the main house and scattered guesthouses (now home of the School of American Research) as well as a narrow and curvilinear water trough bisecting a large patio that became the venue for mock-Mayan rituals staged by Bynner, Mayan scholar Sylvanus Morley and their friends.

In fact, many artists' homes embody a strong sense of theater — a stage for daily life and creativity and also a carefully considered social environment for the artist to interact with others. Even the most private of dwellings, such as Douglas Johnson's "cave" or O'Keeffe's stark hacienda in Abiquiú, has a palpable, literary quality to it.

One remembers Mabel Dodge Luhan's essay in *Winter in Taos* about her sidekick Spud Johnson's Taos home, a cluttered but fascinating workplace jammed with printing presses, newspapers and books, all made into a masterpiece by the overwhelming umber and sienna tones of the studio's Rembrandt palette, which come to life in the raking light of sunrise or sunset.

The influence of the legendary artists' homes of the original bohemian wave in New Mexico still unfolds. It might be said that the second renaissance of New Mexico arts blossomed after 1985, when a real estate boom, Hollywood Westerns (*Young Guns*) and canonization by travel and lifestyle magazines as a great destination combined to attract many more talents to the state.

Megawealth also found its way to New Mexico, and scores of trophy houses are now woven into the serape of the landscape. New Mexico villas like Bynner's or Fechin's are common today — in scale if not audacity.

The creation of luxury and stylish living space in New Mexico has almost become formulaic: sure to include kiva fireplaces, *latilla* ceilings, Chacoan masonry and Talavera tiles! That's why it's refreshing — no essential — that we study and absorb the lessons incorporated in the great homes Emily Drabanski has selected for our enjoyment.

The lifestyle values celebrated in this book are so much more important than techniques of architecture and interior design. They speak to inspired, transcendent living. We are grateful to the artists profiled here for the generous sharing of their homes and lives with us. It's reassuring to know that in the most gifted hands, style is neither static nor stale.

—ELMO BACA

INTRODUCTION

I invite you to step inside some of the most interesting homes in the Land of Enchantment. As the editor in chief of *New Mexico Magazine*, I've been privileged to meet many artists and tour their homes.

These dwellings truly reflect the artists' souls, personalities and creative flair. I find their living spaces to be as inspiring as their artwork. What makes these houses so special? Each artist in this book graciously shared ideas on how he or she created a home that nurtures dreams, offers inspiration and conveys individual artistic sensibilities.

The selection process was difficult since there are scores of talented artists with spectacular houses. I've tried to present a good cross-section of the state's top artists to give you a sense of the variety of homes and décor. At the same time, I invite you to get to know these artists as I have — relaxing with them where they dwell. I have delightful memories of every visit — sitting cross-legged on the floor with Douglas Johnson in his home in a cave, sipping apricot tea with Ford Ruthling as we watched hummingbirds in his garden and talking with Bernadette Vigil about her spiritual transformation.

Although no two artists or houses are alike, I have noted some common themes that lend character, vitality and a more personal, one-of-a kind touch to a home.

While we can't all be successful artists, we can have fun creating a more imaginative living space.

I hope ideas in this book inspire you to envision new ways for your home to reflect your personality and your individual flair.

Convert space – Many artists have converted buildings that very few would normally think of as houses. When you choose an unconventional space, naturally that calls for creativity as you make it into a home. Some examples in our state would include Delmas Howe, who remodeled an old post office in Truth or Consequences; Judy Chicago, who lives in a former hotel in Belén; and Luis Jimenez, who converted a schoolhouse into his home in Hondo.

DELMAS HOWE CONVERTED AN OLD POST OFFICE IN TRUTH OR CONSEQUENCES. THE ECLECTIC DÉCOR INCLUDES A TURKISH KILIM ON THE LEFT WALL, CAMEL BAGS COVERING THE CENTER COUCH AND A MOROCCAN BERBER TATTOO POT ON THE COFFEE TABLE. ONE OF HIS PAINTINGS AND A LITHOGRAPH BY HIM ARE ON THE RIGHT WALL. FOR INFORMATION ON HIS ART VISIT HIS WEB SITE: WWW.DELMASHOWE.COM. (CHRISTOPHER DOW PHOTO)

Use your home as a canvas — For many artists an empty wall or door is just too wonderful to resist. Some paint murals, others add colorful touches or create a trompe l'oeil scene. You'll find examples of this throughout the book. For example, Luis Tapia, known for his contemporary Hispanic sculpture, has added a blue sky with floating clouds to a door. Delmas Howe had fun adding trompe l'oeil scenes, such as a turquoise-sky cloudscape in his small bathroom to give the illusion of being in a bigger outdoor space, as well as a pediment painted above a door to create a more dramatic entrance.

SANTA FE SCULPTOR LUIS TAPIA PAINTED THE DOOR IN THE HOME HE SHARES WITH HIS WIFE, CARMELLA PADILLA, AN AUTHOR. HIS PIECE *DOÑA SEBASTIANA Y SU COSECHA* IS ON PAGE 4. HE EXHIBITS AT OWINGS-DEWEY FINE ART IN SANTA FE. (STEVE LARESE PHOTOS)

reate a sanctuary — Many artists set aside a quiet space for reflection and contemplation. This might be as simple as a *nicho* (built-in shelf or alcove in a wall) that holds a candle or as elaborate as a private chapel. When artists Ed Sandoval and Ann Huston built their home, they built a chapel first. For spiritual author and artist Bernadette Vigil, it was important to incorporate shrinelike areas into her home. Others have set aside an area that contains special personal objects that encourage spiritual reflection.

THIS SHRINE IS A SPECIAL CORNER FOR REFLECTION IN BERNADETTE VIGIL'S HOME NEAR BUDAGHERS, SOUTH OF SANTA FE. SHE LOVES CANDLELIGHT; IN FACT FOR A LONG TIME SHE HAD NO ELECTRICITY. FOR MORE INFORMATION ON THE ARTIST AND HER HOME, SEE PAGE 68. (KIRK GITTINGS PHOTO)

Focus on a fireplace — Most of the artists in this book have a marvelous fireplace that serves as the heart of their home. For some it's a simple hand-crafted adobe hearth and for others it's become another piece of art. Master ceramicist Shel Neymark used his artistic skills to create a colorful corner fireplace that's fun and inviting. Others have added other delightful embellishments, such as the painted trompe l'oeil by artist Pam Platt that gives the illusion of a *nicho* on the upper portion of the fireplace (shown on book cover).

THE COLORFUL FOLK ART OF DENNIS MAGDICH FILLS HIS FORMER HOME IN TESUQUE. HE DESIGNED THE WHIMSICAL FIREPLACE. HIS ARTWORK IS AVAILABLE FROM COLLECTORS ON THE INTERNET. (CHRISTOPHER DOW PHOTO) ON THE FACING PAGE, JOHN NIETO USED BOLD COLORS IN HIS FORMER CORRALES HOME, MUCH LIKE HE DOES IN HIS PAINTINGS, SUCH AS *LONE WOLF* ON THE WALL. HE EXHIBITS HIS WORK AT VENTANA GALLERY IN SANTA FE. (KIRK GITTINGS PHOTO)

Make a splash with color — While some people like the subdued variations of whitewashed walls, others view their homes in Technicolor. I'll never forget walking into John Nieto's home. It was the first time I'd ever seen a home with walls that dazzled the eye with such bold colors as rich purple and deep azure. Miguel Martinez uses strong, intense, yet warm colors on his walls. Dennis Magdich's entire home seemed an extension of his colorful, contemporary folk art.

Anything goes — Perhaps, this is the best tip that I heard from almost all of the artists. They don't hesitate to break the standard decorating rules. None of these artists was concerned with what colors were "in" this year. Most felt comfortable mixing traditional with contemporary looks. All enjoyed surrounding themselves with objects that they felt were beautiful and inspired creativity.

NATIVE

There is no way to describe the typical Native American home today since there is no style that every Indian embraces. Like all other Americans, their homes reflect individual tastes.

Historically the homes of New Mexico's Indians were as diverse as their tribes. Remnants of ancient cliff dwellings give us insight into the people who lived there. Spectacular examples can be seen at Bandelier National Monument and the Gila Cliff Dwellings.

Until the past century, Apaches were nomadic and tepees were practical, portable residences. The Navajos' simple, multisided hogans were efficient for insulating against the extreme summer heat and cold, harsh winters as well as being an outward reflection of spiritual beliefs. Many traditional Navajos still live in hogans, particularly on the Navajo reservation.

The Ancestral Pueblos who lived in Chaco Canyon were some of the Southwest's finest builders. They were meticulous in their placement of doorways and arrangements of carefully layered flat rocks.

Among contemporary Pueblo Indians, many live in traditional adobe homes, others do not. While their homes may be diverse, at the heart of every pueblo a circular kiva serves as a place for ceremonial rituals.

Non-Native Southwesterners today have adopted many Native American design elements into their homes. It's not unusual to find a large, rounded sitting area, inspired by Pueblo kivas, in custom homes. Aspen ladders like those used at the pueblos often add interest to a home's décor. Indian drums are not only played but also prominently displayed or used as tables.

Through the centuries, art has been a way of life

ROOTS

for Southwestern Indians. Ancient remnants of beautiful pottery, carefully carved petroglyphs and intricately woven baskets remind us of longstanding artistic traditions.

Today, R.C. Gorman and Estella Loretto are two successful artists who are inspired by their Native American roots. Both have created homes that reflect their individual artistic sensibilities.

Gorman, who's known throughout the world for his paintings of powerful, maternal Indian women, says his creativity flourished after he had his own home built. A Navajo, whose father, Carl,

ESTELLA LORETTO WANTED A HOME THAT'S CONTEMPORARY YET REFLECTS HER PUEBLO ROOTS. HER SCULPTURE *MORNING PRAYER* LOOKS LIFELIKE. (KIRK GITTINGS PHOTO)

was one of the Navajo Code Talkers, chooses to live in Taos in the shadow of the magical Taos Mountain. Gorman, who loves entertaining, has a spacious home that's comfortable for guests yet provides him with a private studio.

Loretto says her home was built with a blend of Pueblo influences and fine art. Her larger-than-life sculptures animate her landscape. She, too, felt the strong need to create a home that would nurture her as an artist. She lives near Santa Fe within driving distance of the red-rock land of Jémez Pueblo where she grew up.

ESTELLA L⊙RETTO

Sculptor Estella Loretto believes in the power of prayer. So it was important to build a home that would be a sanctuary for reflection, a place to let ideas flow and nurture her artistic life.

She says her spiritual home will always be Jémez Pueblo, but the home where she flourishes as an artist is in the juniper-studded hills north of Santa Fe. The rounded, adobe-style home flows freely from room to room in a shape reminiscent of the Pueblo kivas. "I love beauty and want to surround myself with that which is beautiful," she says quietly.

Carefully painted morning glories and hummingbirds float across the surface of walls covered in warm, hand-ragged, blended earth tones and shades of harvest gold, ocher and harvest red. "I really do not like white walls. I find them cold and sterile," she says. A good friend, Christine Crozier, painted the hummingbirds. Butterflies and hummingbirds are Estella's favorites, and they often appear in her work as well as her home.

"I love all that is feminine. I am a romantic," she adds. So light, lacy curtains and hand-embroidered towels serve as a delightful counterpoint to fine Native American art. Big, round Indian drums double as coffee tables, Native American pottery and carefully woven baskets serve as cultural and spiritual connections more than decorative items in her home.

"I begin every day with a prayer," she says. She prayed long and hard before she bought her land. She sought out the guidance of her late uncle Cristóbal Loretto, who often served as her spiritual guide. He encouraged her to have a home built. "It was not easy. I was a single mom working as an artist, and the financial arrangements were difficult." But she's never regretted the decision.

A new dream was taking shape in the Gentle Spirit Studio adjacent to her home. "I was so incredibly affected by September 11. I was unable to work or concentrate for a few months," she explains. Her own personal healing process began when she learned that Jémez spiritual leaders were invited to go to the site of the World Trade Center for a healing ceremony. "It was very powerful to me that they chose the Jémez Pueblo spiritual healers."

She began working on her largest sculpture titled

ESTELLA LORETTO TAKES A BREAK IN HER STUDIO. IN THE FORE-
GROUND IS A SCULPTURE OF HER MOTHER THAT'S IN PROGRESS.
(KIRK GITTINGS PHOTO)

Prayer for Peace. She had no funding but wanted to create the piece as a gift in remembrance of those who lost their lives, as well as to help others heal. She continues to seek support from legislators and tribal leaders to allow her to complete the work and send it to New York City.

Estella can't remember a time when she didn't love art. "I had art all around me. People were making pottery, and I loved to draw as a child." She was raised with the influence of godparents as well as immediate family and only spoke her native language, Towa, until she was 7.

E STELLA'S ENTRYWAY
SHOWS HER LOVE OF FINE
NATIVE AMERICAN ART.
IN THE FOREGROUND,
THE SCULPTURE
REAWAKENING GREETS VISITORS. ON
THE FACING PAGE, THE VIEW FROM
HER LIVING ROOM INTO HER DINING
ROOM AND KITCHEN GIVES A SENSE OF
THE OPEN FLOW IN HER HOME. HER
SCULPTURE *HUMMINGBIRD DANCE* AND
AN ACOMA POT GRACE THE COFFEE
TABLE. THE SCULPTURE AT THE FAR
RIGHT, *MAGICAL ENCOUNTERS*, WAS
FASHIONED IN THE IMAGE OF HER
DAUGHTER FAWN, NOW A TEEN-AGER.
(KIRK GITTINGS PHOTO)

At 15 she left home to study at the Institute of American Indian Arts. She fondly remembers her teacher the late Allan Houser. "I didn't realize at the time that he would become such a mentor later in my life, but I always had a great admiration for him."

As a teen-ager, she began her exploration of the world with a scholarship to study in Belgium. Before and after studies for a bachelor's degree in ethnic art studies from Fort Lewis College in Durango, Colo., she traveled to study art in Italy, Japan, India, Nepal, Mexico, New Zealand and Australia.

She began her career as a potter and painter. "Growing up in the pueblo, I was so lucky. I had many teachers around me. Some showed me their art, and others shared their

spiritual teachings with me. I was very blessed," she says.

Estella's journey as a sculptor started about 11 years ago. She was preparing an application for a grant and wanted to ask Allan Houser for advice. "He was always a simple guy; he said, 'Meet me at Carrows Restaurant for breakfast.' I wanted to take him to a place like the Inn of the Anasazi, but he said. 'I really prefer Carrows.'" She told him about her dream to become a sculptor. "I asked him, 'Why are there no Native women making monumental sculptures,'" she says. He replied that if someone were going to do it, she'd be the one most likely to succeed. Then he offered to serve as her mentor. "I felt so happy. I knew a lot of people from around the world wrote him letters and asked for his help, so I was honored."

Through his guidance, she prepared her first piece, *Earth Mother*. (The headdress on the 8-foot sculpture has a star in the center – her signature, since her name in Latin means star.) She hoped the piece would find a good home. She says, "He told me, 'Don't worry about it. It will be a great location.' So one day I was driving by the Capitol and I was stunned. There was my piece out in front. It is such an incredible honor to have my work there at the same place that one of Allan's pieces is installed."

Her sculptures grace a variety of locations, including the Institute of American Indian Arts in Santa Fe, the Smithsonian Institution's National Museum of the American Indian in Washington, D.C., and the Heard Museum in Phoenix.

Her dream is to continue sculpting, to help in a healing way through her work. "A large-scale sculpture can have a powerful healing effect on people who come in contact with the work and can even impact a whole environment in a beautiful healing way," she says. "For me, sculpting is a form of prayer."

To contact Estella Loretto, visit her Web site at estellaloretto.com or call (505) 986-8471.

Estella's sculptures, *Earth Mother*, in the foreground, and *Reawakening*, animate her property in this view taken at dusk. This past year she has been working on a sculpture, *Prayer for Peace*, as a gift in remembrance of those who lost their lives in the Sept. 11 tragedy and to help others heal. (Kirk Gittings photo)

R.C. GORMAN

R.C. Gorman has made his home in the Taos area since 1968. The wildly popular Navajo artist's bright and bold paintings of Indian women decorate homes around the world. In fact, his art now decorates vases and ceramic tiles as well as canvases. The flashy artist loves to share his eccentric sense of humor and doesn't hold back in talking about his home.

"It's just my little bachelor pad. I needed it to house my few little art works," he says with a chuckle. Then he adds, "Well, I guess it's not so little. One artist friend calls it Gorman's Palace and another calls it Fort Gorman." It's actually a compound of four buildings.

"I think the main house has 11 or 12 rooms. I'm not sure. I don't have time to count the other rooms like the bathrooms or pantries," he says with a sly laugh.

Rooms that now function as his bedroom and library are more than 200 years old. The rest of the house has been added on to suit his needs. He notes that every ceiling treatment is different: peeled wooden *latillas*, cedar, baffled lighting, sculptured ceilings and skylights sporting etchings by Charles Collins.

When it comes to decorating, R.C. says he doesn't stick to any one style. "There's no particular model or period," he says. He admits to having an overwhelming weakness for works of art, which fill his home.

Skylights and track lighting illuminate the eclectic mix of realistic and abstract art from New Mexico and around the world. A fabric bas relief by New Mexico artist Gary Mauro stretches across a wall where it can be viewed from his large indoor pool. An interesting juxtaposition of *katsinas, santos,* a sculpture of Buddha and a totem pole reflect his diverse tastes in folk art. A Japanese sculpture garden features the work of a variety of sculptors. When asked if he displays much of his own work, he wryly mutters, "Can't really afford it."

The artist remains prolific in producing paintings, bronzes and other works of art that are sought out by collectors around the world. He continues to sell his work through the Navajo Gallery, which he has owned since 1968, in Taos. He has said, "I'm lucky that I can paint as I wish and that people relate to my work in a very personal way. I've always done what is unique to me. I'm starting on my third generation of collectors now, and that means a lot to me."

When not working in his studio, he says he usually gravitates to his living room or kitchen, especially the kitchen. It's no secret that he loves to cook and eat. He's written four cookbooks, *Nudes and Foods*, Vols. 1, 2, 3 and 4, all edited by Virginia Dooley, the director of his gallery. They're everything the titles suggest.

R.C. GORMAN LOVES WORKING IN HIS STUDIO. FOR MORE THAN THREE DECADES HE HAS CREATED ART THAT'S SOUGHT BY COLLECTORS AROUND THE WORLD. (KIRK GITTINGS PHOTO)

It's also no secret that his little bachelor pad is quite a party pad for the gregarious R.C. "I love to entertain. My kind of party is to invite about 500 people and bring in mariachi bands and Aztec dancers."

R.C. has a staff to maintain his home when he travels, such as one trip he took "to have clothes made in Hong Kong, visit friends in Bangkok, do business in Tokyo and unwind in Hawaii."

"But I love coming home," he says. "I never was really successful until I got a good home base. And you know what I really like best about my home? The mountain. Taos Mountain. I can always see it from my home. That's the best part."

R.C. Gorman's art is shown at the Navajo Gallery in Taos, (505) 758-3250; www.rcgormangallery.com.

R. C.'s LARGE DINING TABLE AWAITS HIS GUESTS. HE LOVES TO COOK. ON THE WALL IS A LARGE PORTRAIT THAT HE PAINTED OF HIS FATHER, CARL, WHO WAS ONE OF THE DISTINGUISHED NAVAJO CODE TALKERS. (KIRK GITTINGS PHOTO)

ABRIC BAS RELIEFS ON THE WALL, BY GARY MAURO, CAPTURE THE ATTENTION OF SWIMMERS WHO TAKE A DIP IN R.C.'S POOL. ON THE FACING PAGE, R.C. HAS CONVERTED A HALLWAY INTO A SMALL GALLERY WHERE HE EXHIBITS A VARIETY OF WORK BY NEW MEXICO ARTISTS AND OTHER PROMINENT ARTISTS. (KIRK GITTINGS PHOTO)

ADoBE

When the Spanish arrived in the early 1600s, they encountered Pueblo Indians living in homes made of mud and straw bricks. The Spanish called those bricks "adobe." The word *adobe* has Arabic origins and became part of the vernacular after the Moors invaded Spain.

The Spanish settlers soon began working with adobe to build mission churches and homes. The rituals of mixing mud and straw, molding bricks in wooden frames and plastering with mud soon became an integral part of Hispanic traditions. In those early centuries the building practice was literally dirt-cheap. It required intense labor — something that Spanish settlers and the Pueblo Indians accepted as a way of life.

During the late 1800s and early 1900s when artists from the East first came to northern New Mexico, they fell in love with the mud-plastered homes. They loved the sensuous curves and imperfect edges that seemed such an earthy counterpoint to the perfectly manicured Victorian homes and brick houses that they had left behind.

In the decades that followed, many artists chose to live in adobes, which seemed to spring forth naturally from the environment. Whitewashed adobe walls added to the soothing, peaceful atmosphere that Georgia O'Keeffe and other artists sought away from the bustle of city life. Behind adobe walls on Canyon Road in Santa Fe, artists spent hours painting and having lively exchanges.

Adobe homes' thick walls retained the sun's warmth in winter and kept it cool in summer. The heady scent of piñon wafted from adobe fireplaces. Long sturdy pine log crossbeams called *vigas*

TRADITIONS

supported the roof.

Today, some artists continue to prefer adobe homes. Many build slowly as time and money permit. In the mid-'70s and '80s there was a resurgence of owner-built adobes as many artists became part of the back-to-the-land movement. This included artists who had moved here as well as those with longtime family roots.

Two such native sons, Miguel Martinez and Ed Sandoval, have built their own adobes in northern New Mexico. While their artwork differs, their hand-crafted homes support their cultural roots and creativity.

A VIEW FROM THE DECK AT ED SANDOVAL AND ANN HUSTON'S HOUSE SHOWS THE STONES THAT PROTECT THE ADOBE FROM THE ELEMENTS. (JEFF CAVEN PHOTO)

Artist Ann Huston, Ed's wife, worked alongside him as they built their home. The pastel artist loves painting in an environment in the countryside since most of her work captures rural landscapes. The people of northern New Mexico enliven Sandoval's vibrant paintings.

Miguel, known for his larger-than-life paintings of women of strength, is married to just such a woman, Rita Martinez. She says she always wanted to try her hand at interior design, and their home showcases her artistic sensibilities.

ED SANDOVAL

Contemporary painter Ed Sandoval creates bright, sensuous paintings of life in northern New Mexico. Most of his paintings have a simple adobe church or *casita* in the background.

When he and his wife, artist Ann Huston, decided to build their own home, they wanted a traditional adobe. "Comfortable and simple" are the words both use to describe their preferences.

While the structure is simply elegant, anyone who has built an adobe can see the enormous amount of labor-intensive work involved. With the help of longtime friend Antonio Mendez and his adobe crew, Ed and Ann designed and built their home.

"To me our house is like a fortress — a place of security, peacefulness and sanctuary. Yet it is simple — just made of rock, wood and adobe," Ed says. It has also provided the foundation that has allowed them to pursue their art careers; both have earned many awards and accolades for their work.

Perhaps Ed's most recognized paintings capture pastoral scenes of the northern villages, including those around Taos or Nambé, where he grew up. The majority of his oil paintings are undercoated in red — a signature of his work, which results in rich, intense colors.

Often a *viejito* (old man) appears walking with a cane, much like the lovable character Amarante Córdova in the movie *The Milagro Beanfield War*. Metal sculptures of his character grace the front of their home and gallery.

Ann's pastels on sandpaper typically capture a lone structure, such as an adobe chapel in the dis-

& ANN HUST⊙N

tance on top of a sloping hill. Her serene landscapes often feature a solitary tree and paths that have no beginning or any tangible ending.

She describes her work as "a continuing study of the dichotomy of the human spirit: fragile yet strong, distant but accessible, private and open, always offering us a glimpse of ourselves."

Both she and Ed show their work at their gallery, Studio de Colores, in Taos. It's not unusual to spot Ed's '51 Chevy truck parked out front or to catch either artist at work there.

ARTISTS ED SANDOVAL AND ANN HUSTON WITH THEIR SON JOE STAND BY THE ADOBE BUTTRESS BEHIND THEIR CHAPEL. (JEFF CAVEN PHOTO)

They decided to begin their massive building project by constructing a chapel on their hillside property outside Taos.

"I wanted it to be a special place for us," Ed says. "The chapel has a rock foundation, wooden floors and a wooden bond beam. We looked for old recycled tin to use for the roof. We left the adobe exposed both inside and out. Ann made the cross for the bell tower."

The chapel doubled as a painting studio in the early months but has since become their sacred space. The back of the chapel features a rather large

INES FRAME THE ADOBE CHAPEL THAT SERVES AS A SANCTUARY. (JEFF CAVEN PHOTO)

rounded adobe buttress, which is reminiscent of the famous San Francisco de Asís Church in Ranchos de Taos.

Next Ed and Ann built an adobe home and numerous other structures on the property, eventually incorporating more than 30,000 adobe bricks. They used many traditional adobe building techniques. Most of their home's adobe walls are 26 inches thick. Hefty *vigas* crossed over by *latillas* create a herringbone pattern in the living room ceiling.

The stabilized adobes on the outside of the structure, anchored by a rock cobblestone parapet wall, give it the look of an ancient Pueblo structure. The top roof has a deck that affords a spectacular view of the series of *canales* that drop from one floor to the next to create a waterfall that descends from the house.

Ann selected most of the colors for the interior. She painted all of the kitchen cabinets in shades of turquoise and pale green. "I wanted them to have a warm, cheerful and old-fashioned look," Ann says.

Most of the house features wooden floors over concrete; radiant heat keeps the house warm. In the master bedroom the floor has been painted with a rich turquoise wash.

They have since built a guesthouse that has two
bedrooms, two baths, a full kitchen and living room.
Also of double adobe, it has the same features as the
main house — radiant heat, gorgeous painted pine
floors, three fireplaces, three portals and a hot tub.
While building the guesthouse, an adobe chicken
coop was created, fashioned after Las Trampas
church. Ed jokes about collecting the "holy" eggs.

The landscaping features many private gardens.
Ed and Ann say it was always a tough choice to
decide where to hang out until they added a three-
pool waterfall. For them, the sound of water says,
"Come sit by me!"

The two agree that their home is now finished,
and their creative energy is focused on their painting
careers.

Ann Huston and Ed Sandoval show their works at their gallery,
Studio de Colores, 119 Quesnel, in Taos, (888) 751-3502,
e-mail colores@decoloresgallery.com.

Ann's painting *Ojo Feliz* and an *ofrenda*, a
small wall shrine, flank the kiva fireplace. (Jeff Caven photo)

A SIMPLE, YET ELEGANT ENTRYWAY WELCOMES GUESTS TO ANN AND ED'S ADOBE. ON THE FACING PAGE, THE LIGHT, SUBTLE COLORS ON THE CONTEMPORARY, YET OLD-FASHIONED-STYLE CABINETS KEEP THE SMALL KITCHEN OPEN AND BRIGHT. THE FAMILY GETS A SPECTACULAR VIEW FROM THE KITCHEN WINDOW, WHICH IS SITUATED 30 FEET ABOVE THE GROUND. (JEFF CAVEN PHOTO)

MIGUEL MARTINEZ

W hen Miguel Martinez was growing up in a small house in northern New Mexico, he never dreamed that he'd someday live in a 5,000-square-foot adobe home that's built on favorite stomping grounds from his childhood days.

Actually, square-footage estimates are rough, because there's hardly a piece of his home that is square.

"I had seen a friend's place that was round, and I was immediately drawn to it. And I thought, 'That's what I want,'" the artist says. "Of course, I never knew how much work it would be. Or that a round house requires custom everything — custom doors, windows and you name it."

But the effort paid off. Miguel has created a spacious one-of-a-kind home. The heart of the house is a round tower, similar to the *torreones* built for defense and lookout purposes in early Spanish settlements.

Expansive walls feature the work of many of his friends and other artists who inspire him. The walls also accommodate the paintings for which he is famous — large, powerful images of almond-eyed women of strength and beauty.

"I don't have them around because it's my work. I have them here because I need them. These women give me courage and inspiration," Miguel says, his brown eyes as powerful and engaging as those of his subjects. He also adds that in the early days of his career, he had to sell almost everything he created to support his family. Now he's happy to keep select pieces.

Similar to most owner-builders, he started with a small adobe structure. He credits the help of numerous friends, family members and contractors who lent a hand, and ideas. But after marrying his longtime sweetheart, Rita, who had pitched in to help with the original structure, family and space needs grew.

"We used to have a sunken living room, but that just didn't work with toddlers toppling into the pit, so we filled that in and just kept modifying to meet our needs," he explains with a smile.

"This house is always evolving. It's like a living, breathing piece of sculpture," Miguel says.

All of the walls are adobe. "I love the warmth that emanates. It just feels different from other homes," he says. While their home has been described as beautiful, the Martinezes have taken

MIGUEL MARTINEZ TAKES A BREAK IN HIS STUDIO. (CHRISTOPHER DOW PHOTO)

care that it also feel warm, inviting and comfortable. "It's a house that the whole family really lives in," says Rita, including daughters Danielle and Ciara.

While the home has many spacious rooms, it also has smaller, intimate spaces for reading or quiet conversation.

The artist was the primary designer-builder, but he credits his wife with converting the house into a home. "Everything you see has Rita's touch. She's really wonderful that way," he says as he sweeps his hand across the rooms.

An engaging woman, not unlike the subjects of her husband's paintings, Rita had wanted to try her hand at interior design, and she has filled their home with eclectic furnishings and rugs from New Mexico and their travels around the world to give it a warm, international flavor.

Years ago, Miguel worked as a jeweler, and when he took up painting full time, their space needs again changed. In 1994 each was able to get their dream space: Miguel had always wanted his own large studio and Rita, who had cooked for years in a cramped kitchen, had dreamed of a large, inviting, country kitchen. She dabbles in gourmet cooking and enjoys entertaining.

So Miguel built a separate studio away from the house and converted his old studio and office into a spacious, showpiece kitchen/dining area. Over the stove is a striking example of Miguel's artwork done in tile. Both the kitchen and dining area benefit from a stunning view of Taos Mountain.

Miguel again strove for beauty and comfort in the design of his studio. *Latillas* of split aspen make beautiful cross patterns over the *vigas* of the 14-foot ceilings. The floor in this artist's studio, unlike that in most, is carpeted and then covered with another rug. "It was Rita's suggestion, but she was right. I'm on my legs all day when I paint, so it's worth the effort. Besides, rugs can be cleaned. It also keeps down the dust and makes it a quieter space," Miguel says. As he works, he likes listening to music by favorites such as James Taylor and Ottmar Liebert.

Perhaps the most eye-catching element in their home is the intricate woodwork on doors, shelves and other trim. Among craftsmen who created these features is longtime friend Mark Romero, who created the one-of-a-kind doors and wood accents found in the home. Romero was his neighbor when he was a child, and Miguel always admired his work. "He'll build a door specific to the space, and he'll never make one that looks exactly like that piece again," he says with extreme admiration.

Almost every bit of building material came from the area, which also pleases him. Many of the adobes were made at Taos Pueblo, the wood for *vigas* and *latillas* came from the nearby forests and the rocks for a wall support came from nearby riverbeds.

Miguel Martinez's work is shown primarily in Michael McCormick Gallery, Taos, (800) 279-0879, www.mccormickgallery.com; Contemporary Southwest Gallery, Santa Fe, (800) 283-0440, www.csgart.com; and Adagio Galleries in Palm Springs, Calif., (800) 288-2230, www.adagiogalleries.com.

THE ROOMS EASILY FLOW IN THE ROUND HOME OF MIGUEL AND RITA MARTINEZ. NOTE THE SPOKELIKE PATTERN CREATED BY THE *VIGAS* AND THE HAND-PEELED ASPEN *LATILLAS* AS THEY SPIRAL FROM THE CENTER ROCK COLUMN. WALLS FEATURE WORK BY THE MASTERS AND FAVORITE PIECES OF HIS WORK, INCLUDING *WOMAN FROM RANCHOS* OVER THE COUCH AND *TAMARA* ALONG THE STAIRWAY. (CHRISTOPHER DOW PHOTO)

A STUNNING VIEW OF TAOS MOUNTAIN CAPTIVATES ALL WHO ENTER THE DINING ROOM. THE MARTINEZ FAMILY ENJOYS ENTERTAINING IN THIS ROOM THAT'S A FAVORITE OF GUESTS. NOTE THE HAND-CARVED LEDGE OF THE WINDOWSILL. THE ENTIRE HOME FEATURES AN ECLECTIC MIX OF ART AND FURNISHINGS FROM AROUND THE WORLD AND NEW MEXICO. (CHRISTOPHER DOW PHOTO)

MIGUEL CREATED
AN OIL-ON-
MASONITE
PAINTING,
HOMECOMING, AS
A FOCAL POINT IN HIS SPACIOUS
KITCHEN. A MIX OF TILES PROVIDES
A STRIKING FRAME FOR THE PIECE.
HAND-PEELED *LATILLAS* ADD
INTEREST TO THE CEILING. RITA
ENJOYS CREATING GOURMET DISHES
IN THE ELEGANT YET FUNCTIONAL
KITCHEN. THE CONVERTED SPACE
WAS ORIGINALLY MIGUEL'S FIRST
STUDIO. (CHRISTOPHER DOW
PHOTO)

CLASSIC

In territorial days folks often had a family homestead with several buildings. The structures were frequently behind a wall for defense against Indian attacks and bandits.

Rancho de las Golondrinas in La Cienega near Santa Fe and the Martínez Hacienda in Taos are classic compounds that now serve as living museums. Today we have contemporary reminders in the form of walled patios and secluded courtyards. Artists Michael Hurd and Ford Ruthling are among those who live where a collection of buildings — a compound — still exists.

Landscape artist Michael Hurd lives on the southern New Mexico ranch of his parents, renowned artists Henriette Wyeth and Peter Hurd. The Hurd property, the Sentinel Ranch, is named for a hill where a sentinel would watch for bandits and fire three warning shots if he saw intruders.

Today hidden gardens and a walled Mexican-style courtyard at the ranch ensure solitude for Michael when he paints and for guests who rent *casitas*. By lovingly restoring and updating their compound, he's kept memories of the family's historic ranch alive.

As a youngster, Michael Hurd was also exposed to the northern New Mexico art scene. He vividly recalls one gathering. "I was just 6 and I had to wear a suit. That was awful at that age. I could smell and see all this wonderful food when I came in, and I was so hungry. I also saw a rather austere woman standing nearby, and I saw lots of big paintings of flowers, skulls and clouds. Well, I reached for the food and my mother quickly scolded me and told me I'd have to sit outside in my dad's old Suburban. I remember saying to my mother, "I don't care, the party is boring and the art is just awful." He says his family

COMPOUNDS

roared because the woman with the big flower paintings was Georgia O'Keeffe.

Santa Fe artist Ford Ruthling was also exposed to the burgeoning art scene in his youth, but some of his fondest recollections are of time spent in nature.

He grew up in Tesuque with his

PETER HURD'S FREQUENT TRIPS TO MEXICO INFLUENCED THE DESIGN OF THE WALL AND COURTYARD. (KIRK GITTINGS PHOTO)

the University of New Mexico in 1952 where one of his instructors was Randall Davey. In 1954, he joined the Air Force Aviation Cadet program, and upon completion of the program, he returned to Santa Fe to work as an artist.

Ruthling never lost his love of nature and in the '70s pur-

immediate family and his mother's parents. He loved being surrounded by a lush landscape that featured strong, sturdy apple trees, and he felt nurtured by his grandparents. Though as a youngster he began sketching and was primarily self-taught, he attended

chased a compound in Santa Fe. The property was originally for tuberculosis patients and ultimately housed pregnant teens. Today, his artistic hand has created a colorful adobe compound, which embraces an enclosed garden.

MICHAEL HURD

The tall, lanky landscape painter Michael Hurd wears jeans and cowboy boots, much like his dad, artist Peter Hurd, did. As he walks the grounds of Sentinel Ranch in the verdant San Patricio Valley of southeastern New Mexico, he recalls the story his father told him about bringing his bride to the ranch for the first time.

Peter, born in Roswell in 1904, attended West Point and went on to study with prominent painter N.C. Wyeth. During his 10-year stay in the East, he fell in love with N.C.'s daughter, Henriette Wyeth — that was in the late 1920s.

Peter, however, longed to return to the West, so his bride agreed that he'd go and get a place ready. About a year passed before Peter would pick up Henriette at the Carrizozo train stop. "They say it was a beautiful moonlit night, and when she saw the place with its whitewashed walls, she thought it was incredibly beautiful. Of course, the next day when the sun came up, the condition of it was quite a revelation to my mother. My dad was used to the bachelor's life, and the ranch was pretty rudimentary. At that time there were no phones and all the power came from a generator," he says. She was accustomed to the life in the East but quickly fell in love with the solitude and beauty of the area, as well as the people.

The couple shaped the home into a welcoming hacienda filled with a mix of ranch furnishings, pieces from Mexico and furniture from the East. They often painted sunup to sundown. While they needed solitude to paint, both enjoyed entertaining. *Casitas* housed many guests, such as actress Helen

Hayes, who came to have portraits painted.

Having lost both his parents — Peter (at 80 in 1984) and Henriette (at 89 in 1997) — Michael has refurbished the property, developed guesthouse rentals and built a gallery that features the family's artwork.

Visitors can now stay in the renovated Wyeth house or in other *casitas*. While it retains its rural ranch flavor, the Wyeth house now has modern amenities.

MICHAEL HURD STANDS IN HIS STUDIO, BUILT BY HIS FATHER, PETER HURD, IN THE 1930S. TWO RAMS' HEADS FROM A NORMANDY, FRANCE, ABBEY FLANK THE LARGE HAND-CARVED DOORS FROM MEXICO. (KIRK GITTINGS PHOTO)

Michael lovingly restored his mother's home. He made sure that the lower half of the kitchen walls was painted with a dusty rose paint wash, just as his mother did. He's kept the original 1930s hardware on doors. He had new wooden floors installed but was able to retain the original *vigas*. Kitchen cabinets made in the '50s were painted a deep forest green, while white ceramic tiles behind the stove surround tiles with a green shamrock design in honor of the town of San Patricio's namesake, St. Patrick. He incorporated pinks and greens in the house because those colors often occurred in his mother's work.

A comfortable sitting room has a kiva fireplace and window that's low to the ground that was a door in the original structure, which was part of the Maes family homestead in the 1850s.

THE UPDATED KITCHEN RETAINS THE ORIGINAL *VIGAS* AND THE 22-INCH-THICK ADOBE WALLS FROM THE 1850s HOMESTEAD. MICHAEL SAYS THAT THE CEILINGS WERE PLASTERED BETWEEN THE *VIGAS* YEARS AGO TO KEEP HEAT IN AND DUST OUT FROM THE 6 INCHES OF EARTH ON THE ROOF. THE OLD COPPER POTS HANGING ON THE WALL RACK WERE USED BY HIS MOTHER, HENRIETTE WYETH. (KIRK GITTINGS PHOTO)

Outdoor patios beckon visitors to enjoy the fresh air. From the king-size bed covered in a country-style blue-and-white quilt, one can see the sunroom. The kitchen door opens to a Mexican-style courtyard.

Just behind the home a footbridge crosses the original acequia named after Margarita Maes, the homesteader's daughter that some say was Billy the Kid's girlfriend. A path leads to a garden that has a gazebo given to Peter Hurd by prominent oilman Robert O. Anderson.

Michael paints oil landscapes in his dad's studio. He works from original field sketches or watercolors, eschewing photographs. The studio has a big fireplace with tiles inlaid with some of his dad's favorite humorous Spanish expressions.

Seeing his son's practical abilities, Peter suggested he study business. Michael graduated from Stanford University and worked for a while in industrial real estate. He also performed with the New Kingston Trio.

His dad encouraged him to return to run the family ranch and Michael says his business background helps him keep the 2,400-acre spread operating. "While my dad always encouraged me to explore the world, he told me that all roads lead to art."

Michael then studied art at New Mexico State University. His mother was a tough, but constructive critic. "I remember once when I had just begun a life drawing class, she reviewed a nude study I had done. She looked at it and said, 'Oh, the poor dear. Is her right arm really 4 inches longer than her left?'" Today his parents' spirits linger. Every building, tree and plant has a story. "For me, it's just as important to preserve this environment as it is to preserve the home."

He found a source in Mexico and replaced more than 6,000 terra cotta tiles on the hacienda roof. He laughs when he says, "The originals came from La Luz, near Alamogordo, and the story is that the pieces were shaped around the thighs of a rather large woman there until she got tired of making them."

Among the many buildings that his father built was "the orangery," a lush, enormous greenhouse. Michael repeats the story about two visiting Los

Alamos physicists who drank dry martinis in the orangery one night. Suddenly they saw two tiny lights moving through the flowerbeds and then cross one another. "Well, my father says they swore off drinking and were sure they had the dts. My father had put candles on the backs of two turtles. He had a good laugh," he says.

"I had the world's best education right here in San Patricio. There were always lively conversations about science, literature and the arts. I learned much from my godfather, Paul Horgan (prominent New Mexico author)," he adds.

When asked if it was a delightful place to grow up as a child, the artist, in his mid-'50s, grins with a twinkle in his eye and says, "It was, and it still is."

To see Michael Hurd's art or for information about guest rentals, call Hurd La Rinconada Gallery, (505) 653-4331, (800) 658-6912 or visit the Web site at wyethartists.com.

H ENRIETTE WYETH USED THIS BEDROOM UNTIL SHE DIED. THE ADJACENT SUNROOM WAS BUILT IN THE 1990S. THE FACING PAGE SHOWS THE PORTAL. THE CHEST IS FROM MEXICO. THE HATS BELONGED TO HIS FATHER, PETER HURD. MICHAEL SAYS HIS FATHER RODE HIS HORSE MOST AFTERNOONS, OFTEN CARRYING HIS PAINTING SUPPLIES. (KIRK GITTINGS PHOTOS)

FORD RUTHLING

Open the turquoise gate at the Santa Fe compound of New Mexico-born artist Ford Ruthling and you'll feel like a child who's discovered the secret garden. Amble through the house, and at every turn you'll feel as if you've either entered a European chapel or somehow followed Alice through the Looking Glass. You've definitely entered a magical space.

His home oozes with Santa Fe charm and, probably more importantly, with the personality of a true Santa Fe character. The heady scent of oil paints permeates the air and the sound of Ford pounding tin punctuates the sound of classical music playing loudly in the background.

A well-established painter, he also produces colorful folk art-inspired pieces from tin, creates fine drawings and has had his designs incorporated into large harvest bowls made in Mexico. In 1977 a series of his paintings of Pueblo pots became U.S. postage stamps.

Ford has added his colorful touch and building skills to his home, furnishings and gardens. His work is collected by people around the world and is in several museum collections.

"Being an artist is all about creativity and imagination. I'd hate to be one of those artists who just repeat the same type of work over and over again. I always want to be trying to do something that's new. I guess the only thing I haven't done is sculpting; maybe I'll try that next," says the 70-year-old artist. "I'm always a painter first, yet I love to draw the human figure. It's the thing I like to do most. Also, I love nature and you can see that in my work."

In his studio, an iridescent, outsized cobalt blue butterfly fills a large canvas. A richness of texture and shimmers of light evoke the beauty found in nature. In addition to bird and insect life in his garden, an extensive butterfly collection is under glass in a library coffee table.

Ford's love of nature permeates his garden and rambling

FORD RUTHLING TAKES A BREAK ON HIS PORTAL. HIS STRIKING TINWORK GRACES THE COLORFUL DOOR. (KIRK GITTINGS PHOTO)

of the feeder. "Oh, that's great, the hummingbirds are back," he says with a childlike grin. His garden is compact, yet filled with brightly colored flowers that vie for space with his colorful glass and tin garden lights. Inside the house, bouquets of fresh flowers bring a kaleidoscope of color into his already rainbow-colored *casa*.

His home has all the charm and eccentric-

adobe *casa*. Two dogs and a cat roam about freely — his dogs Molly and Jack rarely leave his side. On a summer afternoon Ford sits in a wrought iron chair on his portal as he speaks while watching birds dart from flowerbeds to birdfeeder.

He identifies each species as it sits on the perch

ities of older adobes. The floors are deliciously uneven, yet lovingly covered with an array of well-worn Oriental rugs. Worn layers of paint on the wooden kitchen floor reveal a mottled collage of blue, yellow and orange. Never mind that the sea green kitchen cabinets don't match the floor.

Nothing does, and with good intention. The home has all the richness and chaos of nature.

Colorful folk art vests cover pillows on his couch to give the illusion of an international gathering of men. He crafted the large, stately whitewashed headboard for his bed by piecing together parts of an old Mexican bar counter, topped off with a triangular pediment Throughout, he's incorporated an eclectic mix of furnishings that comes from flea markets, antique dealers and world bazaars.

"I really don't like to be called a collector," Ruthling says as he rolls his eyes. Yet one can easily see that his home is filled with fabulous collections. It's chock-full of religious artifacts — fine examples of New Mexico *santos*, as well as reliquaries and processional pieces that he's found in Europe and Mexico. "I'm not a Roman Catholic,

R ELIGIOUS ART FROM NEW
MEXICO, EUROPE AND
MEXICO FILLS THE LIVING
ROOM. THROUGH THE
DOORWAY IN THE FAR
RIGHT CORNER, ONE OF FORD'S PAINTINGS,
OF A COLUMBINE, IS VISIBLE. ON THE
FACING PAGE, FORD'S WORKSHOP FOR HIS
TINWORK IS ADJACENT TO HIS PAINTING
STUDIO. (KIRK GITTINGS PHOTO)

ONE OF FORD'S CREATIONS, A GLASS-AND-TIN WEATHER VANE IN THE SHAPE OF A FISH, TOWERS OVER HIS ENCLOSED GARDEN. HE LOVES SPENDING TIME IN THE GARDEN AND FEELS INSPIRED BY THE WORKS OF BEAUTY HE FINDS IN NATURE. THE ENCLOSED GARDEN SERVES AS FORD'S PRIVATE SANCTUARY FOR REFLECTION AND RELAXING. (KIRK GITTINGS PHOTO)

but I have a true appreciation and fascination with this type of folk art," he says. Indeed, the glass-covered case embedded in the dining room table that reveals a Christ Child figure from a Mexican Nativity set has surprised some of his dinner guests.

Ford's interest in folk art landed him a job as a curator at the Museum of International Folk Art in the mid- '60s. Although he doesn't get to travel as much as he would like, when he does, he seeks out indigenous work. He is drawn to pieces from Latin America and is now seeking interesting African work.

While he's mainly self-taught, he is captivated by the work of the early European masters. "I'm probably most impressed with the work of Albrecht Dürer. I love his work with the human form. His drawings and etchings are so inspired."

"I admire a lot of other people's work, but I get my greatest inspiration from works of beauty in nature." He says it's akin to his own belief system that revels in nature and imagination. "I'm struck by the wonder of a butterfly, well-crafted

writing, the voice of an accomplished opera singer — and all that's creative, imaginative, inspired."

His home, his garden and his artwork all convey his sense of wonder and creativity.

As he ages, Ford says he appreciates Georgia O'Keeffe's desire to be reclusive. "I was much more sociable, but now I want my private time for my garden, my work and my personal life."

Indeed, a sign in his driveway warns "Beware of owner." He no longer exhibits his work in a Santa Fe gallery, but he does show his work by private appointment. Please phone ahead. Otherwise, if you drop by, he'll gruffly ask you to leave. But like his dogs, you'll find his bark is worse than his bite.

To contact Ford Ruthling, call (505) 982-2241.

LIVING

An artist's home provides intimate sanctuary. The size of that sanctuary is not as important as its being a place for solitary reflection as well as deep connection to the natural environment. Such is the case for both Bernadette Vigil and Douglas Johnson, who choose to live simply in a way that has minimal impact on the land. Their hand-crafted homes support and ignite their creativity.

Though their work is quite different, one senses interesting ties in their environments and art. They live in remote locales where one can feel both the tranquility and the tremendous power of nature. One often sees endless turquoise skies that kiss the earth at dawn. As the sun sets, an occasional double rainbow paints the vista or lightening flashes to the beat of heart-stopping thunderclaps. These are not places where nature is taken for granted. When the velvet darkness of night enshrouds their homes, they light candles as part of a daily ritual. Moonlit nights invite them to walk outside to the call of coyotes. Nature is an integral part of their palette.

While the landscape could seem stark and harsh to an outsider, many artists' works capture the rich and vibrant colors of the peoples and environments of the Southwest. Vigil and Johnson have done this successfully in bold and captivating ways. Vigil's work often reflects the love of her Hispanic heritage. Near her hand-crafted home is a longtime family chapel. In recent years many family members have moved close to her once isolated home.

Johnson, too, is drawn to the cultures of New Mexico, having lived in close proximity to Indian tribes and traditional Hispanic villages, as well as its spiritual connections: He's created more than two dozen paintings of traditional adobe churches. As

SIMPLY

someone who hauls his own water and lives without electricity, he can relate to a more historic lifestyle. And not unlike some earlier Indian inhabitants, he chooses to live in a "cave."

Vigil and Johnson have furnished their homes in simple ways. Some artists discover that a freedom from material possessions gives them freedom to create. The late Georgia O'Keeffe displayed cow skulls, bones and stones in her beloved Abiquiú, the

DOUGLAS JOHNSON LIVES SIMPLY IN HIS CONVERTED CAVE. NOTE HIS CHILDHOOD TRAIN ALONG THE LEDGE. (KIRK GITTINGS PHOTO)

décor of a simply furnished home. One of New Mexico's greatest contemporary artists, Agnes Martin, has a home just as open and spare.

Even though some New Mexico artists do live in spacious homes or have elaborate studios, others live in trailers or paint in spaces that some people might see as sheds rather than studios. Most of these artists would say that small is beautiful.

For Vigil and Johnson, living simply is a choice, not a hardship.

DOUGLAS JOHNSON

Douglas Johnson has found sanity in simplicity. His days revolve around essential rituals — drawing water from a nearby spring, carefully using the least amount of wood to build a fire. Every act of living becomes Zenlike, from making a cup of tea to working on his latest painting.

His home, fabricated from rocks and other natural materials, hugs the boulders near Coyote, west of Abiquiú. Inspired by the Anasazi Indians as well as the philosophy of Frank Lloyd Wright, Johnson sought to build a house that works with nature, not against it.

"First of all, I love rock," he says. "But I also wanted to build a house that would be the least intrusive. You need to extend nature around you and wrap it around yourself.

"My house is living art. You build an environment and then you live art everyday. I didn't learn how to paint until I came here. I never went to art school, and I never had time to pursue art until I isolated myself here. What has taught me is the natural world."

Reclusive by nature, Douglas values privacy. Although recent years have brought him success, he has no intention of bringing electricity or running water to his home. He *chooses* the simple life. Perhaps the first thing one notices about his house is its small scale. Entering through a low, narrow door, it's as though one has followed Alice into a small Wonderland. The dimensions are smaller than some ancient Indian cliff dwellings — and it seems a perfect fit for Douglas.

"I built this house for me. I always intended to

live here. I didn't build it to sell to someone else … it's the way I wanted it," he says.

"I have no architectural background, but I was inspired by the ruins at Chaco Canyon. I saw what had been done and said if it worked for those people, it could work for me."

Douglas, who has an engaging sense of humor, laughs at modern buzzwords. "People started writing books about how to use solar energy. The people in Chaco Canyon were using passive solar energy before books were being written. Other people tell me I'm an environmentalist. But I lived this way before there was a word for it. I just use what I need. It's simple."

His lifestyle makes monks seem self-indulgent.

DOUGLAS JOHNSON LIVES NEAR COYOTE, WHERE HE FINDS MUCH INSPIRATION IN NATURE. (KIRK GITTINGS PHOTO)

His only lights are candles and kerosene lamps. He uses only five gallons of water a day, bathes out of buckets and produces about two garbage cans of trash every six months. "It's really easy to live this way."

Of Douglas' artwork, David Turner, former director of the Museum of Fine Arts, noted, "The world of Douglas Johnson is quiet, elegant and orderly. Through his small-scaled paintings, he helps the viewer escape, as he has, from a modern world too often guided by chaos to a more serene, personalized space."

This passage could also describe the interior of his home. Natural objects and hand-crafted items from world travels line the rock shelves in a highly

organized fashion. There's no clutter — just a precise collection of objects rich with detail: Thai ceramics, Burmese lacquer ware and woodcarvings from Bali.

Furnishings consist of sparse, functional pieces. He sits on a tiny bench alongside the fireplace as he speaks. A comfortable, overstuffed chair seems to be set aside for guests who might feel unaccustomed to the rocky environment.

Rockwork walls that seem to be dull shades of gray and brown, on closer inspection reveal rich coloration and sensuous lines as well as seashells and pottery shards. Ceilings sport hefty spruce *vigas* and aspen *latillas*; a Navajo Yei rug hugs the floor.

The shepherd's bed on a rock shelf serves as a guest bed in the living room, and a Pueblo-style ladder leads to Douglas' bedroom. A sweeping, curved boulder that serves as an interior wall also offers natural shelf space. A small train from his childhood days wends its way around the gentle curve of the wall. Fascinated by trains, Douglas frequently incorporates them into his work.

Bright splashes of red and black glimmer from

DOUGLAS' HOME BLENDS IN WITH THE NATURAL SURROUNDINGS. ON THE FACING PAGE, A MIX OF STONES FROM THE AREA WAS USED TO BUILD THE WALLS. HE ALSO HAS AN ADOBE STUDIO NEARBY WHERE HE CREATES INTRICATELY PAINTED WORKS THAT DEPICT ASPECTS OF THE STATE'S MULTICULTURAL HERITAGE. HE LOVES TRAINS AND FREQUENTLY INCORPORATES TRAINS INTO HIS PAINTINGS. (KIRK GITTINGS PHOTO)

the tile work on windowsills. And as a man who has few indulgences, he snickers about his red and black Ralph Lauren bedding.

In a tiny dining nook, above a marble-top table, he displays a collection of paintings of saints in antique tin frames. The floor features Oaxacan brick floors and Talavera tile. The window ledge holds 40 different types of miniature cacti.

What appears to be ancient Anasazi pottery basks in the sun on a kitchen windowsill. These are his dishes — pots he made himself in the traditional Indian way.

While Douglas lived among the Navajos as a VISTA volunteer in the late '60s, an elderly woman showed him how to find and prepare clay, then shape it. He learned to polish and fire bowls using cow dung.

"I came to the Navajos and learned from them. And when I moved here, the Spanish-Americans came to me and I learned from them," Douglas says. He created an adobe studio, incorporating traditional Hispanic building methods.

The people of New Mexico touch his life in many ways, perhaps most profoundly in his approach to painting. Based on the Navajo method of weaving while sitting on the floor, he has rigged his easel so he can sit on the floor to paint. "It also helps me to get the type of detail that I want in a small space," Douglas explains.

He describes his work as surrealist and humorist. "But don't try to categorize my work because it always changes. It has to. I don't believe in copying myself," Douglas says emphatically. "I'm not into success and power. I'm only interested in creating better work. I'm never quite happy with any of my work. I'm obsessed with perfection."

His studio is closed to visitors. Since he only works with natural light, his hours for painting are precious and few. Besides, he's a recluse. If his pit bulls don't discourage visitors, he says the rattlesnakes usually do.

Douglas Johnson exhibits his work at Nedra Matteucci Galleries in Santa Fe (505) 982-4631 www.matteucci.com and Parks Gallery in Taos (505) 751-0343 www.parksgallery.com.

Upstairs in Douglas' bedroom, the rock ledge holds an eclectic mix of objects, including a San Juan dough bowl, a Tarahumara bowl, Thai teak carvings and a Oaxaca mescal jug. The bedroom is only accessible by climbing a Pueblo-style ladder. He says the inspiration for his home comes from the ruins at Chaco Canyon as well as the philosophy of Frank Lloyd Wright. (Kirk Gittings photo)

BERNADETTE VIGIL

Every aspect of artist Bernadette Vigil's home feeds her soul. "Some days it reminds me of a temple and other times I feel like I can retreat into it like a cave," she explains as sunlight streams in from the skylight.

Working with help from friends and family, Bernadette designed and built the circular home in the wide expanses of ranch land near Budaghers between Albuquerque and Santa Fe. The property is part of the homestead of her mother's parents, Pablo and Dolores Leyba. "My grandfather was a miner in Madrid and my grandmother pretty much ran the ranch," she explains.

Her grandmother, no longer living, was a great inspiration to her. "She was incredible. Most of the small pieces of furniture around here were made by my grandmother. She could ride horses and just about do anything that needed to be done on the ranch," she says.

Though many of her paintings include rich, intense colors, her home has primarily subdued tones that echo colors of the surrounding foothills. Simple, stair-stepped adobe walls separate the rooms and allow light to travel throughout the house. A large pyramid skylight in the roof provides natural illumination.

"The light out here is a precious gift. It has greatly influenced my work. I see light in a totally different way," she says. While she keeps a studio in Santa Fe, she also spends many hours painting right in her living room, particularly in summer.

For many years she had no electricity, so she used only candles. This, too, affected her work.

"When the candlelight is dancing and the stars

glow overhead, it brings a total reverence into the space," Vigil says. Much of her artwork has a deep, spiritual quality.

Bernadette grew up on Canyon Road in Santa Fe, where she felt the influence of the dynamic art community. Her early works, from the 1980s, painted in oils or acrylics, focused primarily on portraying life in traditional Hispanic rural villages, drawing inspiration from her family roots.

In the mid-'80s, she studied buon fresco. Painting with the technique, which uses freshly ground pigments on wet plaster, she created colorful murals in Santa Fe and Albuquerque. She says that several of these projects provided excellent opportunities to work with at-risk youth.

It was during the '90s that she began studying

BERNADETTE VIGIL STANDS OUTSIDE HER CIRCULAR ADOBE. (STEVE LARESE PHOTO)

Toltec wisdom, studying for 11 years as an apprentice to the shaman *don* Miguel Ruiz, author of the best-selling book *The Four Agreements.* Her artwork began to reflect that spiritual transition in her life. Images of the six directions and the raven, which has a strong personal, spiritual connection, dominate her more recent paintings.

In addition to her work as an artist, she's become a recognized spiritual author and teacher. Writing as *doña* Bernadette Vigil with Arlene Boska in *Mastery of Awareness: Living the Agreements*, she tells about her own spiritual journey and gives advice on how others can make personal transformations. Today she travels around the world offering Toltec wisdom workshops. Regarding her writing, she says, "It's just another aspect of art. You

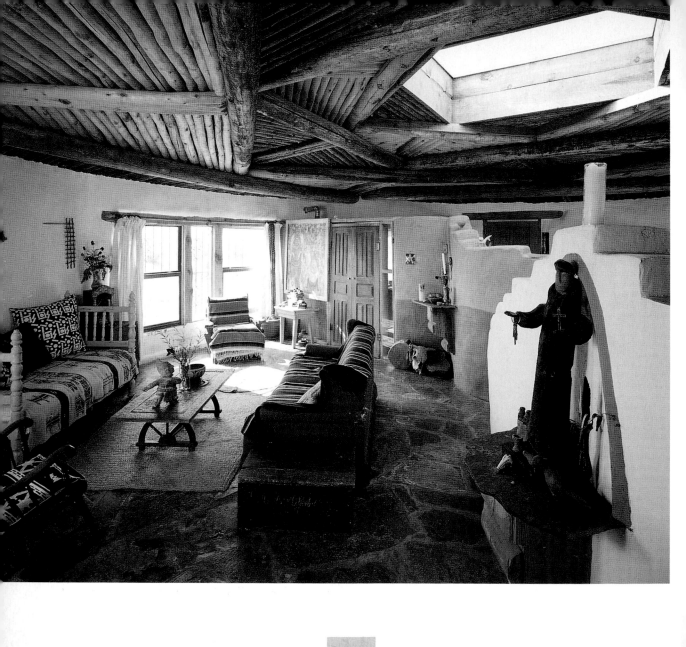

An overview of Bernadette's living room. Hand-peeled *latillas* stretch across the *vigas* in the round home to create a pattern that some say reminds them of a basket. A pyramid skylight scatters light through the house. Her home near Budaghers, south of Santa Fe, is on ranch land that was part of her mother's parents' homestead. (Kirk Gittings photo)

should never limit your ability of expression."

She's currently writing a book about awareness for children. She continues to go on pilgrimages to South America and India to continue her spiritual development. But in New Mexico her home remains her sanctuary.

Small collections of artifacts — shrines of various sorts — fill the corners of her home. Frequently she keeps sage burning in one of these spaces. An array of beautifully shaped rocks rests along her adobe walls. She uses these for meditation.

Almost everything in her home was either given to her or received in trade. An old, carved small table was a gift from the well-known eccentric artist Tommy Macaione, who died in 1992.

Simple objects — baskets, crosses, skulls and Indian drums — become works of beauty in her hand-crafted space. An old, worn wooden adobe-maker provides a shelf for more treasures, which include her baby shoes and family photos.

Like many owner-built adobe homes, hers seemed to grow organically. A reddish beige mud from nearby La Bajada shades the base of the wall.

A wagon wheel frames a view of the Jémez Mountains from her kitchen. Hand-punched tin plates with Corn Maiden designs cover her kitchen cabinets.

But perhaps the most remarkable aspect of her home is found overhead. An incredible crisscrossed ceiling of hand-peeled *latillas* creates an intricate geometric pattern between the *vigas*. "Some people have said it reminds them of a basket," Bernadette remarks.

In recent years, she's added a strawbale addition that has two bedrooms, a bathroom and another living area for guests or workshops. She has retained its original round form. "I'm still living with the elements and living the simple life," she says.

Bernadette Vigil's artwork is represented by LewAllen Contemporary Gallery in Santa Fe, (505) 988-8997, www.lewallen.com

A FLAGSTONE FLOOR CONTINUES FROM THE LIVING ROOM AREA INTO THE BATH. WE GET A BIRD'S-EYE VIEW OF TWO PEOPLE ON HORSEBACK IN HER PAINTING ABOVE THE TABLE. IN THE FAR RIGHT, THE CORNER SERVES AS A SMALL SHRINE. ON THE FACING PAGE, HER BEDROOM FURNISHINGS RETAIN THE AMBIANCE OF HER GRANDPARENTS' RANCH. (KIRK GITTINGS PHOTO)

FUN &

Perhaps the most intriguing aspect of entering an artist's home is the element of surprise — the idea that almost anything goes. Combine that with the spirit of people who enjoy having fun and laughing at life and you'll enter a home that emanates a resounding *joie de vivre*.

Almost all the artists in this book have some part of their home that is either funky or fun. Sometimes the funky elements are a result of having creatively used what was available or simply sprung from the artists' own outrageous artistic expression. These homes were definitely not decorated by Martha Stewart.

Lively accounts of New Mexico's early artist colonies in Santa Fe and Taos include colorful details of the lively and sometimes raucous gatherings in artists' homes. Today a number of artists still

take a break from solitary lifestyles to host a friendly bash in homes or back yards. Metal sculptor Thom Wheeler in Taos looks forward to such get-togethers. An apple orchard surrounds his home and provides all the ingredients for his famous cider-making parties. Painters Elias Rivera and Susan Contreras like to invite friends for an evening of food and dancing, especially after completing work for a new exhibition. In Taos, R.C. Gorman says he likes to bring in a mariachi band and Aztec dancers to throw a party for a few hundred friends.

Wheeler, who creates what he refers to as "wall jewelry," scours flea markets and sales looking for interesting architectural details for his owner-built adobe castle. When visitors arrive, they ring the bell that came from one of the old boxing rings at Madison Square Garden. Large pillars that frame the entry of the master bath were once part of a funeral home. Wheeler clearly had fun building his

FuNKY

house and calls it his largest piece of sculpture. While the home has fine details that reflect Wheeler's precise woodworking skills, it is a comfortable place where kids, cats and dogs feel right at home.

The dogs definitely feel at home in artist Tavlos' Santa Fe *casa!* Tavlos, who was thrust in the spotlight in the mid-'80s with his humorous and colorful howling coyotes, shares his home with his wife, Pamela Preston, and oodles of

COLUMNS FROM A FUNERAL HOME CREATE A DRAMATIC ENTRYWAY INTO THOM WHEELER'S BATHROOM. HIS ECLECTIC FURNISHINGS GIVE HIS HOME A FUN LOOK. (KIRK GITTINGS PHOTO)

poodles. The beautiful show dogs have free rein in Tavlos' home. If Wheeler's home is a sculpture, Tavlos' is a painting in progress. A rainbow of hand-painted designs brighten cabinets and doorways throughout.

Ubiquitous coyotes contribute splashes of color and whimsy, and Tavlos' large acrylic paintings that document the mythical adventures of his sly and cunning coyote character Sonny Boy further reveal Tavlos' fun-loving sense of humor.

THOM WHEELER

Sculptor Thom Wheeler's towering adobe in Taos reminds some of a castle. In fact, Wheeler has a real fondness for medieval times.

Thom also has a longtime love affair with New Mexico, although he grew up in Texas. The successful metal sculptor created many large commissioned pieces that sold rapidly in Texas during the oil boom. When the economy slowed and Thom felt a need for a simpler lifestyle, he chose Taos.

He first purchased a small Victorian in the mid-'80s and decided to build an adobe studio. When it grew to a grand scale — 38,000 adobes — he sold his other home and moved into the adobe castle.

"This place grew like one of my sculptures," Thom says with his lingering Texas drawl. "And it's still growing. I spent almost two years full time working on it. And I'll probably always be making modifications and improvements."

He has always loved building and designing. His father was a shipbuilder, who worked mainly on yachts. So from an early age, Wheeler was around woodworking and metal work.

"I built this in a lot of ways like you would build a yacht. Everything's sealed and secure. I'm ready for any great floods," he says with a laugh.

He's not exaggerating. Every cabinet and door is finely finished and sealed. Though it's an expansive home, there's no wasted space. Wooden benches surround his kitchen table and double as yacht-style storage cabinets.

Thom peruses flea markets, garage sales and auctions. Many of his found treasures serve decorative as well as useful functions in his home. The large teak front door is from Vienna, Austria. Many of the windows came from an old schoolhouse in Texas. And large pillars near the master bath are from an old funeral home. If the front bell looks like the kind used for boxing matches, it's because it came from a training ring at Madison Square Garden.

Subtle touches reveal Thom's fascination with Moslem designs. Several windows and *nichos* have peaked arches, and he's incorporated simple flowing geometric designs in tile work throughout the house.

An expansive studio downstairs in his home accommodates the artist's large-scale pieces. As a metal sculptor, he works with bulky, heavy pieces of equipment. So it's not surprising that the studio rests on an 8-inch-slab supported

THOM WHEELER RESTS ON ONE OF THE WOODEN BENCHES HE DESIGNED. ABOVE HIM IS HIS PIECE *TURTLE DANCER*. (KIRK GITTINGS PHOTO)

by three tons of steel. His work requires the 16-foot-ceiling, which has supporting *vigas* made from enormous Wheeler Peak Ponderosa pine.

The connotation of metal work might make one think his home could be cold or impersonal. But it's not. It's vibrant with light, plants, pets and personal touches, such as lace curtains. The consummate collector displays toys that are more than 50 years old and pieces of cowboy kitsch.

Since moving to Taos, his work has taken on a New Mexican flavor. *Katsinas* and conquistadors show up in his work in addition to his popular cowboy pieces.

"I like to think of my work as wall jewelry," Thom says with a big grin. His sculptures dazzle the eye with multifaceted polished bronze, brass, aluminum and copper textures that incorporate stones, gems and even crystal doorknobs.

The studio provides the perfect backdrop for his wall jewelry. His giant metal *Cowboy Rainbow* stretches above a massive fireplace and other pieces catch the light and draw attention to the walls.

Unlike other artists who keep their studios closed, his front door at 939 Kit Carson Road is often open to browsers. When he's unavailable, he locks the gate to the property with a chain.

"I never used to see the people who bought my work. Now I frequently meet them when they stop in my home. I like the connection. I enjoy knowing where my work will go," Thom says.

He never regrets his move to New Mexico. In fact, his business is booming. Sales have been so good for Thom that he and his partner, Donna Brunton, opened the Zane Wheeler Gallery, which is named for their 5-year-old daughter, Bailey Zane, on the Taos Plaza. In addition to his artwork for residences, he enjoys designing and creating large-scale works for corporations and public buildings, often collaborating with prominent architects.

Even with growing business, Thom carves out time to return to work on his house — an ever-changing sculpture. After his adobe castle was completed, he decided to build what he calls "his gingerbread Victorian studio." The building, just 30 feet from his main studio, is used for carpentry and foundry preparation. Other recent projects include an outdoor waterfall.

He mentions that he was impressed to see homes built by artists, such as Nicolai Fechin, when he moved to Taos.

"I have a lot of pride in Taos. And maybe someday, a couple of hundred years from now, this will be a historic house, too."

Thom Wheeler's work can be seen at his Zane Wheeler Gallery in Taos, (505) 751-7220, and on his Web site, www.thomwheeler.com.

A N OVERVIEW OF THOM'S LIVING AREA AS SEEN FROM HIS KITCHEN. HIS CATS AND DOG FIND COMFORTABLE RESTING PLACES AMID THE ECLECTIC COLLECTION OF ANTIQUES. NOTE THE LARGE *VIGAS* HE USES AS CEILING SUPPORTS. (KIRK GITTINGS PHOTO)

THE SPRAWLING DOWNSTAIRS SERVES AS THOM'S MAIN STUDIO. HIS PIECE *COWBOY RAINBOW* STRETCHES ACROSS THE MANTEL ABOVE THE FIREPLACE. ON THE TABLE ARE A NUMBER OF HIS PIECES IN PROGRESS. WHEN THE FRONT GATE IS OPEN, HE INVITES VISITORS TO COME IN. THROUGHOUT HIS STUDIO YOU CAN SEE A NUMBER OF HIS METAL SCULPTURES, WHICH HE REFERS TO AS "WALL JEWELRY." HE LOVES MOORISH DESIGN AND THAT'S VISIBLE IN THE SHAPE OF WINDOWS AND IN THE *NICHO* ON THE BACK WALL. (KIRK GITTINGS PHOTO)

TAVLOS

"Art is a celebration of color" is Santa Fe artist Tavlos' credo. "I'm fond of saying I want color in my life (he pauses) and then I need even *more*," Tavlos says with a laugh. Some might say he sees with kaleidoscope eyes as he peers through his purple-rimmed glasses. In his artwork, mountains may be green, clouds pink and the land purple. And no one can miss his vibrant coyotes that come in a rainbow of colors, including neon.

Oh, those coyotes. They've brought him popularity and income as well as disdain from those who felt the howling-coyote phenomenon took over the Santa Fe art scene.

He knows the question is coming, so when asked, he gives a mischievous grin so often found on his most famous coyote — Sonny Boy — and shrugs his shoulders. "I'm really sorry about all that." He never imagined that everyone would begin selling miniature coyotes, howling coyote T-shirts and knickknacks. Obviously, many of these blatant copies of his work were a far cry from the care and energy that he puts into his artwork.

While others have created a cheesy stereotype image of his beloved coyote, it is a very personal symbol for him. About 17 years ago he lost his wife, Sharon, to a brain tumor. The time that followed was filled with dark nights punctuated by the eerie sound of remorseful, howling coyotes. In 1986 he met Pamela Preston, who brought love back into his life and a grin to coyote's face. Suddenly, he heard the coyotes' playful songs and calls to laughter, rather than mournful cries.

His character Sonny Boy isn't simply a howling

coyote; he's often a sly, comical character in Indian headdress and cowboy boots that has a penchant for sensuous women.

According to Tavlos, the signature of his work is the hard-edged black line that defines his Southwestern images. "That black line keeps everything together. I like strong color and colorful imagery of the Southwest." It's an interesting juxtaposition of desert and cultural themes — coyotes, Koshare clowns and even Our Lady of Guadalupe can inhabit his art.

When it's time to kick back from his work in his studio and gallery on Guadalupe Street, he heads home to the foothills north of Santa Fe to his latest hideaway, which he built with much design consultation from Pamela.

THE ART SHOWCASED IN HIS GALLERY REFLECTS TAVLOS' LOVE OF COLOR. (MARK NOHL PHOTO)

The home is not only filled with his artwork but with his colorful touches on cabinets, doorways and anyplace that he deems might otherwise look drab.

Colorful throws from Mexico drape comfortable red couches in the living room. A glass table juggles on the noses of four of his howling coyotes.

Floor-to-ceiling windows at both ends of the living area provide sunlight for a profusion of plants and embrace views of the Sangre de Cristo and Jémez mountains, as well as the surrounding juniper-studded foothills.

He loves the New Mexico vistas because they remind him of Greece — without the ocean. Born in Alton, Ill., he was raised as a first-generation Greek-American and says his childhood was filled with the sounds of Greek from family and friends. When he took the family's last name as his own, it wasn't his attempt to be a megastar like Madonna or Cher, but it was an attempt to stop pronouncing his first name, Dionysios, for everyone. He treasures his Greek roots.

Having lived in New Mexico for 30 years, he's just as enamored with the state's beauty and cultural diversity. He wears a chunky silver and turquoise tourist bracelet that he loves, and his eyes sparkle when he talks about attending Indian dances.

The property where his house stands is near land once owned by Joseph Bakos, one of Santa Fe's famed Cinco Pintores. These artists embodied the free spirit of Santa Fe's early art colony. Bakos became a good friend to Tavlos when he came to Santa Fe, and it was through Bakos that he acquired a piece of property to build his first house. "It was an exchange of paintings and some cash, truly a gift from one artist to another," Tavlos explains.

He first saw the Southwest when he was stationed with the military in El Paso and knew he would return. Like so many artists, he struggled in the early years. He remembers nervously going to R.C. Gorman's Navajo Gallery in Taos with his work. "To my surprise, he liked my work," Tavlos says. It was his first break into the gallery world, and Tavlos showed his work at the Navajo Gallery throughout much of the '70s.

Today the treasures displayed throughout the house look like a cross-section of the New Mexico Museum of International Folk Art collection and items from Santa Fe's famous flea market. "I admit it — Pamela and I are the king and queen of kitsch," Tavlos says with a wry grin.

If they are the king and queen of their castle, it's no doubt that their eight show poodles are the princes and princesses. "I generally like dogs better than most people," he acknowledges.

If you visit his gallery, you'll probably run into one of the poodles, and the fun-loving artist will no doubt give you a Tootsie Pop for dropping by.

Tavlos shows his work at Tavlos Gallery, 405 S. Guadalupe, (505) 820-2828. www.tavlos.com

A PAINTING OF A HAND (30 INCHES BY 22 INCHES, ACRYLIC ON MASONITE) AT THE TOP LEFT IN THE KITCHEN IS PART OF HIS *KACHINA GIMME FIVE SERIES*. *THE VALENTINE CUPID: PAMI AND TAVI* (26 INCHES BY 16 INCHES, ACRYLIC ON MASONITE) HANGS OVER THE STOVE. TAVLOS HAND-PAINTED THE COLORFUL CABINETS. (MARK NOHL PHOTO)

THE TWO PAINTINGS IN
TAVLOS' LIVING ROOM
ARE PART OF HIS *BEASTIE
LOVE SERIES.* TAVLOS'
SIGNATURE COYOTE
HOWLS. ON THE FACING PAGE, A 39-
INCH BY 90-INCH ACRYLIC ON CANVAS
FROM THE *BEASTIE LOVE SERIES* DOMI-
NATES THE HALLWAY. THE TITLE
READS *THE TEMPTATION ACCORDING TO
SONNY BOY: HAVING BEEN OFFERED THE
FORBIDDEN FRUIT BY EVELYN, KNOWN TO
ALL AS EVE, SONNY BOY'S THINKING THIS
IS NOT PARADISE LOST. THIS IS IT. THIS IS
PARADISE. THIS IS BEASTIE LOVE. OH-H-H-
H. LOOK OUT.* (MARK NOHL PHOTO)

SPECTACULAR

While artists' homes nurture their spirits, most find they need a private place to create — a studio. This could be as small as a special table or easel or as large as a separate building.

Within that space, artists build an environment that's functional, and yet fosters creativity. In almost cocoonlike fashion, this hideaway separates them from the distractions of the household.

Probably the greatest common denominator for artists is the need for natural light. For decades, New Mexico's clear light has been a beacon drawing artists here. Large windows and skylights bring in that magical illumination. For those inspired by our mystical landscape, windows also often serve as a conduit for connection with the natural world.

Although there are many similarities, each workplace truly reflects the individual's needs for inspiration. Some artists work in a silence broken only by the sound of paintbrushes swishing on a canvas, a pot turning as the potter works a wheel, or the foot pedals tapping on the weaver's loom as a shuttle slips gently to and fro. Some work reflectively to recordings of classical music while others play rip-roaring rock 'n' roll. Some work with meticulous order, while others have sketches and art supplies strewn about.

When artistic couples share a household, they sometimes also share a studio, though create separate work areas to accommodate individual needs.

After painters Elias Rivera and Susan Contreras upgraded and renovated their Santa Fe-area home, their next priority was to have individual studios. They worked closely with their builder to design two self-contained buildings that would meet each one's

STUDIOS

needs. Both joke about how separate studios have saved their marriage but, more seriously, they acknowledge how their mutual support and individual studios have nurtured them in a way that has inspired creativity and productivity.

For weaver Nancy Kozikowski and her husband, John Cacciatore, owner of the Dartmouth Gallery, creating a studio was integral to the remodeling process of their home in Albuquerque. Kozikowski needed suitable space for dyeing and hanging her

A WALL WITH LARGE GATES, FEATURING ORIGINAL 1930S HARDWARE, TIES TOGETHER THE HOUSES COMBINED BY NANCY KOZIKOWSKI AND JOHN CACCIATORE. (KIRK GITTINGS PHOTO)

yarns and even more room to set up several large looms as well a space for her pastel painting. In their case, instead of creating completely separate areas, they concentrated on working with an architect to connect two small homes into a larger compound.

Like other couples who go through the remodeling process, both couples endured years of living life to the rhythm of hammers pounding and saws singing. Neither pair was able initially to buy their perfect dream house, but both created environments where their dreams can come true.

ELIAS RIVERA &

When you walk into Elias Rivera and Susan Contreras' home, you're struck by bright, intense colors and a decidedly Latino flavor that can be seen in the furnishings of their adobe home as well as their canvases. Elias, who moved to Santa Fe in 1982, primarily paints large-scale works in oil that vibrate with the shapes, colors and exuberance of life found in the marketplaces of Mexico and Guatemala. His other passion — woodworking — has filled their home with handmade tables and cabinets. Susan's playful artworks capture the festivities and follies of life often found at the circus or a masquerade ball. Indeed, the walls of their home are filled with almost as many masks as most of her paintings are.

Elias and Susan share much in common yet admit they grew up world's apart. Elias, of Puerto Rican descent, spent most of his life in New York and easily speaks a New Yorker's lingo. Susan was born in Mexico City. At age 5 she was thrust into the English-speaking world in California. She says her mother's penchant for travel led to an almost gypsy-style childhood that took her to homes in London and Madrid, as well as sojourns in Seattle and Canada. As a teen-ager she lived in Switzerland until the family moved to Santa Fe.

After high school she studied photography with Todd Webb, then art in schools in California before going to the Skowhegan School of Painting and Sculpture in Maine. She moved back to Santa Fe in the early '80s. Not long after, she met Elias, who was seriously ill with a kidney disorder.

"I was pretty close to dying," Elias says, "and

SUSAN CONTRERAS

fortunately I was able turn my life around through nutrition, alternative healing and my renewed interest in art. I had burned out on the art scene in New York and just didn't have a place there. I was drawn to classic art forms and everyone tried to get me to be something else." His subsequent recovery, aided by much enduring love from Susan, led to a new vitality for life that took him on trips to Mexico and Guatemala — now the subjects of most of his work.

PAINTERS ELIAS RIVERA AND SUSAN CONTRERAS RELAX IN THEIR LIVING ROOM. A PORTION OF SUSAN'S MASK COLLECTION COVERS THE WALL. (KIRK GITTINGS PHOTO)

Susan says her reaction to the house was almost like her response when she first met Elias. "It was not exactly love at first sight," she says with an impish grin. "But I truly love both now." Speaking about their house, she says, "Elias fell in love with this place immediately. He loved both the rounded shape of the house and the surrounding five acres. I looked at it and said, 'The well is not very good, the place really has no heat and the roof needs fixing!'"

Elias, who had sold his brownstone in New

York, was enthralled. "This place really spoke to me. It said, 'This is your place.' And the property was so delicious," he says referring to the land where their *casa* is nestled among the junipers and piñons northeast of Santa Fe.

The renovation process initially focused on making the house more livable. Typical of many traditional adobes, there wasn't any closet space. So they knocked out a wall to create a small room that Susan refers to as "a dream walk-in closet."

Today, with most of the remodeling completed, the home has a cozy feel with an eclectic mix of furnishings. The two say it's pretty easy to see their influences. "I love leather chairs and fine art," Elias says. Susan adds with her delightful laugh, "I'd have to say anything that is folk art and fun is something I've picked out."

While Elias likes elegant furnishings, she explores flea markets and garage sales for treasures. Some things appeal to both of them — such as Jim Griffith's whimsical wood sculptures and the enormous dining table Elias built, which serves as the focal point for entertaining.

"We knew we had to build separate studios," Susan says. "In the studio we're opposites: I love chaos and have paints, notes and canvases everywhere. Elias loves to keep his neat and orderly."

Each studio has expansive wooden porches that look like inviting retreats. "My studio got built first. And when I saw it, I thought I'd died and gone to heaven," says Susan, who had worked primarily in cramped spaces. The studio is bright and airy with windows that embrace the view of birds that flit from tree to tree. Assorted masks and antique windup toys vie for space inside.

Elias' studio is larger to accommodate his giant canvases. He has an elegant bathroom with marble and gold fixtures, as well as a space with a bed to crash on when he's working on a major project. "One of the most ingenious suggestions the Tapia brothers (Daniel and Earnest of Deerhorn Construction) made was to build a loft," he says. "From there I can really get a better perspective on my large paintings." Also in the loft is a small office and tidy rows of CDs for his extensive classical music collection.

"I am so grateful; every day we say how lucky

A LOFT ABOVE ELIAS RIVERA'S STUDIO AFFORDS HIM A GOOD OVERVIEW OF HIS LARGER-THAN-LIFE OIL PAINT-
INGS AS WELL AS THE NEARBY FOOTHILLS. THE PAINTINGS OF A FLOWER MARKET IN GUATEMALA WERE EXHIB-
ITED IN 2002 IN A MUSEUM SHOW IN VERONA, ITALY. HE ENJOYS THE SPECTACULAR VIEW OF THE MOUNTAINS
FROM HIS STUDIO. (KIRK GITTINGS PHOTO)

I N SUSAN'S STUDIO, PLAYFUL MASKS
APPEAR ON THE WALL AS WELL AS
IN HER PAINTINGS. ON THE FACING
PAGE, BUSTER, A FOLK ART STATUE
FROM NORTH CAROLINA, SEEMS
TO TAKE IN THE VIEW OF THE KITCHEN
AND DINING AREA. (IT IS ONE OF SUSAN'S
FAVORITE FLEA MARKET FINDS.) IN THE
FOREGROUND IS A TABLE THAT ELIAS MADE.
A WATERCOLOR BY SANDY GOINS AND A
CAST-IRON MASK FROM IRELAND GRACE
THE KITCHEN WALL. (KIRK GITTINGS
PHOTOS)

we are to be in this house and have our studios. It took a lot of time and money, but it has paid off," says Susan, who has enjoyed more than 20 years working as an artist. Elias has become one of Santa Fe's most distinguished artists with exhibitions abroad, as well as in New Mexico.

Elias Rivera exhibits at Riva Yares Gallery in Santa Fe, (505) 984-0330, and you can also see his work at www.rivayaresgallery.com. Susan Contreras shows her art at Hahn Ross Gallery in Santa Fe (505) 984-8434 and Parks Gallery in Taos. (505) 751-0343. For information visit www.hahnross.com and www.parksgallery.com.

NANCY KOZIKOWSKI

Nancy Kozikowski's Albuquerque home seems artfully woven into the tapestry of her life, as artfully woven as her bold, contemporary weavings, which grace the walls of museums, top corporate headquarters and homes.

She feels she's come full circle. She grew up in the same neighborhood where she now lives with her husband, John Cacciatore, owner of the Dartmouth Street Gallery. Their remodeled Albuquerque home is actually the combination of two small houses, a wonderful compound that serves as living space as well as a studio for her weaving and painting. The interior, filled with rugs and tapestries from around the world, reflects Nancy's love of weavings, while John's aesthetics resonate in the juxtaposition of contemporary art and technological accouterments, such as state-of-the-art computers and sound system.

"This neighborhood means a lot to me," Nancy emphasizes. She explains that she comes from a long line of visionaries, builders and supporters of the arts. "I grew up thinking everyone remodeled. We were always knocking out a wall and renovating. Then we'd move to the next place." Her grandfather, A.R. Hebenstreit, was a prominent Albuquerque developer. "He could look at a space and see the future," she adds.

"When I look at my neighborhood, I see through my grandfather's eyes," Nancy says. "Others come here and see an old neighborhood. I see a wonderfully developing area between downtown and Old Town with wonderful places such as the zoo, aquarium and museums."

The early years of her weaving career took her

far from the city lights. She was first married to another prominent artist, Janusz Kozikowski, and they lived in the rural northern New Mexico community of Medanales near Abiquiú, where they raised their children, one of whom, David, also chose to become a weaver.

NANCY KOZIKOWSKI PAINTS AND WEAVES IN HER STUDIO, WHICH IS ADJACENT TO THE ROOM WHERE SHE DYES HER YARN. (KIRK GITTINGS PHOTO)

that "they are all artists who have developed their own styles and cultivated their own traditions." Although their marriage ended, Nancy still has great respect for her former husband.

A few years ago one of her pieces was in an East Coast museum show. She was unable to attend the weaving exhibition, but she found out that her weaving was the only one from the Southwest. Outraged, she organized a contemporary Southwest weaving exhibition in 2001 at the Albuquerque Museum that featured the work of 25 weavers. "I could not allow these weavers to go unrecognized," she says.

"Weaving is such a family tradition in New Mexico. It's all about working in your home," Nancy says. She points out the long traditions of weaving in Hispanic and Navajo households.

During the '70s and '80s the Kozikowskis trained dozens of weavers at their Medanales studio. Many of the state's top weavers got their start there. "We taught the basics," Nancy explains, but notes

Nancy has made a point to meet other weavers and to learn about their traditions. She worked closely

S KEINS OF COLORFUL DYED YARN HANG IN THE SUN TO DRY. THE FORMER KITCHEN WAS CONVERTED TO THE DYE ROOM. THE HOME IS FILLED WITH NATURAL LIGHT SO SHE CAN SEE THE PRECISE COLORS OF THE YARN. (KIRK GITTINGS PHOTO)

with Ramah Navajo weavers on the Fourth Phase Chief's Blanket that was installed in the Statue of Liberty in 1986. "Most people have no idea how much is involved in Navajo weaving. They raise the sheep, dye and spin the wool, build a loom and then weave. It's a year-round process," she says.

The home she's renovated with her husband has many features that accommodate her needs as a weaver. "How many homes do you know that have three kitchens?" she asks with a laugh. But one is strictly used to dye yarn. And their compound, which might seem spacious to many, was quickly filled with three full-size weaving looms. "I have the materials for at least a dozen looms. So I often need a lot of space for different projects," she says.

"We just did not have enough room in the original house, but I wanted to stay in the neighborhood. So I made an offer to a neighbor who was ready to sell, and we bought the house next door. Of course, I was ready to knock out walls and go to town, but this process made

John really nervous," she says.

When he argued that they needed a plan before going any further, Nancy answered that she had a plan. "I had drawn it out with a stick in the dirt," she laughs.

But at her husband's encouragement, they enlisted eminent architect George Pearl and a team from Garrett Smith architectural firm to help them transform their streetscape into a cohesive unit rather than having it appear as two disconnected homes.

They had a large front room and dining room but wanted a more open look. Pearl suggested old-fashioned roll-up garage doors, of glass. It seemed like a wild idea, but it works perfectly. The design allows them to open both sides so people can stroll through the front walled yard as well as the sculpture garden in the back. "It's turned out to be a fabulous place for family wedding receptions," Nancy says.

To brighten up the space, the home now has 23 skylights. She says it's critical to see the subtle differences in the colors in her dyed wool.

"I really loved this place because it was so old,

and we tried to retain that feeling wherever we could," Nancy says. The traditional adobe structures had all the charm — *vigas*, wooden floors and solid adobe walls. But they also had all of the drawbacks, such as very few electrical lines, no closet space and dark interiors.

Their remodeled home retains much of the original adobe interiors, with beautiful wood flooring and striking *vigas*. The old sections intersect cohesively with updated sections that feature stained concrete floors warmed by Nancy's collection of rugs from around the world.

Both admit that the remodeling took much more time and money than expected, but they say it was worth it. They now have the perfect house for weaving tapestries — and dreams.

You can see Nancy Kozikowski's work at Dartmouth Street Gallery in Albuquerque (505) 266-7751 or (800) 474-7751, or logon to www.dsg-art.com. One of her most spectacular pieces, Runways, is on exhibit at the Albuquerque airport.

THE CONVERTED DEN/OFFICE STILL RETAINS THE ORIGINAL *VIGAS* AND HAS A MORE TRADITIONAL LOOK. THE LARGE CHARCOAL DRAWING IS BY ROBERT WALTERS, AND THE LITHOGRAPHS ARE BY GARO ANTRESIAN. THE WINDOW SHADE IS ONE OF NANCY'S HAND-DYED TAPESTRIES. ON THE FACING PAGE, NANCY'S BRIGHT, BOLD CONTEMPORARY WEAVINGS ON THE WALLS SERVE AS AN INTERESTING COUNTERPOINT TO THE ANTIQUES, TAPESTRIES AND RUGS FROM AROUND THE WORLD. (KIRK GITTINGS PHOTOS)

CONTRIBUTORS

Elmo Baca, who wrote the foreword, is a native of Las Vegas, N.M., and was educated at Yale and Columbia universities. Elmo has written numerous books and articles on New Mexico's dynamic heritage and often presents lectures on topics of architecture, design, heritage, tourism and development. Some of his most popular books include: *Santa Fe Design, Native American Style, Rio Grande High Style: Furniture Craftsmen* and *Romance of the Mission: Decorating in the Mission Style*. Baca is former New Mexico State Historic Preservation officer (2000-2002) and served for four years as director of New Mexico's Main Street program. He currently divides his time between homes in Chimayó and Santa Fe.

Jeff Caven has created imagery for architects, construction companies and resort communities in New Mexico for 17 years. For the past decade, he has also been producing a special portfolio of artists at work. He says the photography for this book draws on all of these experiences. He adds that he appreciates this opportunity to represent the state of New Mexico in the media. One of his sunset images was used for the cover of the *2003 New Mexico Vacation Guide*.

Christopher Dow says, "I view each assignment with an artist's eye. It's in my background; my mom was an artist and my father was a photographer." Through his business View I, he has photographed subjects from architecture to fashion. His images have appeared in *Architectural Digest, California Homes, Interior Expressions* and other publications. Through the years, he's made frequent visits to New Mexico and decided to become a Santa Fe resident this past year.

Kirk Gittings, a 45-year New Mexico resident, is an architectural photographer working for major local and national magazines; he is an instructor at the School of the Art Institute of Chicago and the View Camera Workshops and an adjunct professor at the University of New Mexico. The fine arts photographer is represented in many leading private and museum collections. A 30-year retrospective of his fine-art photography opens in 2003 at the Paul Paletti Gallery in Louisville, Ky.

Steve Larese is *New Mexico Magazine*'s associate editor, photo editor and photographer. His work also has appeared in *National Geographic Traveler*, *Sunset*, *Art & Antiques*, *The Boston Globe*, *The New York Times*, *USA Today* and other national publications. "Helping with this book inspired me to paint my own walls in reds, purples and greens, and the effect is stunning," he says. "It doesn't take much time or money to drastically improve your home, just guts and creativity, as these artists show."

Mark Nohl, a native of Santa Fe, was staff photographer for *New Mexico Magazine* and the New Mexico Department of Tourism for 25 years. He currently works as a free-lance photographer. His photographs have been published around the world and his fine-art prints have been displayed in numerous exhibitions across the country. He is currently represented by Photogenesis: A Photography Gallery and Contemporary Southwest Galleries, both in Santa Fe, as well as by Blackstone of New Mexico in Albuquerque.

ACKNOWLEDGMENTS

I'd like to acknowledge all those who helped make this book possible, particularly the artists, who graciously opened their doors to me. I am grateful to the book's designer, Bette Brodsky, who has presented the material in a fun and interesting way. I thank Ree Strange Sheck, whose skillful editing helped shape the book. I appreciate the support from my husband, John, throughout the project.

Elmo Baca, who wrote the foreword, has shared his love and enthusiasm for architecture and design with *New Mexico Magazine* for years. He generously gave encouragement and feedback to me.

I thank all of the *New Mexico Magazine* staff. Their support has meant a great deal to me. I am particularly grateful to Linda Sanchez, who assisted with a variety of tasks, and Walter K. Lopez, who proofread the book.

Since a picture's worth a thousand words, I appreciate the talented photographers, who spent countless hours photographing these homes. I give special thanks to Kirk Gittings, whom I consider the principal photographer. It was because of his enthusiasm and a portfolio of artists' homes that he showed me in the early '90s that I began my exploration of artists' homes.

—EMILY DRABANSKI

GLOSSARY

banco: bench, often of adobe, along a wall

canales: roof downspouts that project out of a wall

latilla: small saplings between beams in ceilings, placed in varied patterns

katsina: a small carved figurine representing a Hopi deity

kiva fireplace: corner fireplace, often in a beehive or modified-beehive style

nicho: recessed space in a wall often used to hold a statue or other artwork

portal: long porch or covered walkway with the roof supported by posts

vigas: horizontal wooden roof beam that may project beyond surface of exterior walls